New Vanguard • 58

Medieval Siege Weapons (1)

Western Europe AD 585–1385

David Nicolle • Illustrated by Sam Thompson

First published in Great Britain in 2002 by Osprey Publishing,
Midland House, West Way, Botley, Oxford OX2 0PH, UK
443 Park Avenue South, New York, NY 10016, USA
Email: info@ospreypublishing.com

CIP Data for this publication is available from the British Library

ISBN 1 84176 235 0

Editor: Simone Drinkwater
Design: Melissa Orrom Swan
Index by Alan Rutter
Originated by The Electronic Page Company, Cwmbran, UK
Printed in China through World Print Ltd.

06 07 08 09 10 10 9 8 7 6 5 4 3

FOR A CATALOGUE OF ALL BOOKS PUBLISHED BY OSPREY MILITARY AND
AVIATION PLEASE CONTACT:

NORTH AMERICA
Osprey Direct, C/o Random House Distribution
Center, 400 Hahn Road, Westminster, MD 21157, USA
E-mail: info@ospreydirect.com

ALL OTHER REGIONS
Osprey Direct UK, P.O. Box 140,
Wellingborough, Northants, NN8 2FA, UK
E-mail: info@ospreydirect.co.uk

www.ospreypublishing.com

Artist's Note

Readers may care to note that the original paintings from which the colour
plates in this book were prepared are available for private sale. All reproduction
copyright whatsoever is retained by the Publishers. All enquiries should be
addressed to:
Sam Thompson, Eikon Illustration, Eikon Ltd., 170 Upper New Walk, Leicester
LE1 7QA
The Publishers regret that they can enter into no correspondence upon this
matter.

Author's Note

For the 'Class of 2001'
Clare College, Cambridge.

MEDIEVAL SIEGE WEAPONS (1) WESTERN EUROPE AD 585–1385

INTRODUCTION

Siege warfare dominated military operations in most of western Europe throughout the Middle Ages, so it is no surprise that the medieval period was amongst the most inventive and varied when it came to the development of non-gunpowder military machines. It was also an age which saw the existing military-technological traditions of the Graeco-Roman world, Iran, India and China being brought together. Medieval western Europe participated in this fusion of knowledge, though largely as a receiver rather than as a provider of ideas. In terms of siege technology the most inventive civilizations were those of China (see New Vanguard, *Siege Weapons of the Far East* 1 & 2) and the Islamic World (see New Vanguard, *Medieval Siege Weapons (2) Byzantium, The Islamic World & India*).

The emphasis placed on technological aspects of siege warfare reflected, and was reflected by, changes in military architecture, giving Europe those superb castles and urban fortifications that survive today to draw tourists from around the world. But almost nothing survives of the remarkable machines which medieval armies constructed when faced by such castles and city walls. There are, however, written descriptions, a few technical treatises which are difficult to interpret, and numerous usually very simplified illustrations.

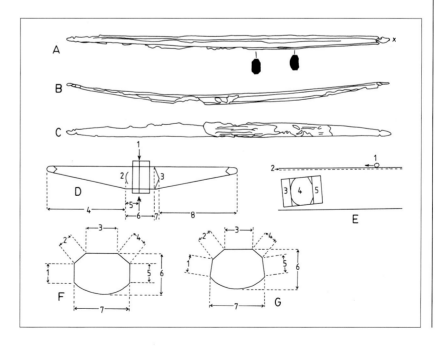

The Berkhamstead Bow is from a large form of siege-crossbow, probably mounted on a wooden frame or rested upon a wall. It dates from the early 13th century and is made from a single stave of wood. A: The back of the bow with two cross sections. B: The top of the bow. C: The front of the bow. D: Schematic reconstruction of the bow mounted slightly off centre on its stock; 1 – centre line; 2 – indented apex of mark at bow centre; 3 – raised apex of mark at bow centre; 4 – 54.8 cm; 5 – 6.7 cm; 6 – 15 cm; 7 – 1.3 cm; 8 – 52.3 cm (After R.C. Brown). E: Cross section of the bow and its attachment to the stock: 1 – bowstring on the surface of the stock; 2 – groove for bolt or quarrel; 3 – wedge; 4 – bowstave mounted at a slight angle; 5 – plate (After R.C. Brown). F: Cross section through the centre of the bowstave: 1 – 1.3 cm; 2 – 1.1 cm; 3 – 3.1 cm; 4 – 1.2 cm; 5 – 1.6 cm; 6 – 3.8 cm; 7 – 5.4 cm (After R.C. Brown). G: section through the bowstave 43 cm from end (see X): 1 – 1.6 cm; 2 – 1.2 cm; 3 – 2.6 cm; 4 – 1.2 cm; 5 – 1.7 cm; 6 – 3.8 cm; 7 – 5.2 cm (After R.C. Brown). (Royal Armouries, Leeds, England)

Most early medieval fortifications either consisted of Late Roman walls or of recently constructed earth and timber structures. These latter could be highly effective and were well able to cope with existing siege machines. Nevertheless, as these machines got more powerful, accurate and reliable, there was an almost universal move from earth and timber to stone and brick defences. The so-called Twelfth Century Renaissance with its amazing cathedrals, great castles and huge expansion of agriculture also saw major changes in the number, size and complexity of siege machines which depended upon much the same basic technology. In several respects Italy led the way, partly because of its close trading relations with the advanced civilizations of the Islamic and Byzantine eastern Mediterranean, and partly because the skills demanded of an experienced military engineer were very similar to those demanded of a naval architect or sea captain. Such knowledge travelled far and fast, but there were setbacks, as when a Scottish force tried to use a mangonel against the castle of Wark in 1174, only succeeding in sending a stone straight upwards to fall back upon one of its own men. In the 13th century German expertise in siege technology gave the Baltic Crusaders a huge advantage over their pagan foes, yet the importance of military engineers did not stop them being regarded with distaste by many in the European aristocratic élite. This attitude was summed up by an early 13th-century French poet, Guiot de Provins, who complained: 'Did Alexander have sappers, or did King Arthur use siege engines?'

On the other hand rulers mostly recognised their usefulness, and possession of such sophisticated weaponry was reserved for those with considerable power. Another reason why governments were generally able to keep control over heavier siege equipment was the enormous cost of

'The Expedition of Holofernes' in the 11th-century Catalan Roda Bible. Several defenders are using staff-slings. These had been used in many parts of Europe since at least Roman times and operated on essentially the same principle as the earliest forms of beam-sling mangonel. (Ms. Lat. 6, f. 134r, Bib. Nat., Paris)

its manufacture and maintenance. The materials involved often also had to be brought considerable distances. For example the Calendar Close Rolls records of England refer to timber for three 'balistas' being ordered from the Forest of Dean 'for Edward, the King's Son' in 1257. During the English siege of Stirling in Scotland in 1304, materials came from all over England while the mayor of Newcastle upon Tyne, a major seaport, also sent four men and one woman to make ropes for the engines. Meanwhile in France the great Clos de Galées in Rouen not only made ships for the French king during the 14th century, but also manufactured siege machines along with astonishing volumes of arms and armour.

'The Siege of Damietta during the Fifth Crusade' in the Historia Major of Matthew Paris, English c.1240. Two Crusaders in the stern of their ship have staff-slings. These weapons were often used to throw containers of incendiary material. (Ms. 16, f. 55v, Corpus Christi College Lib., Cambridge)

During the Middle Ages the transportation of bulky pieces of siege equipment always remained a problem. Draught animals and, more rarely, heavy wagons had clearly carried materials for siege warfare during the early medieval Carolingian period, but the rugged terrain of regions like southern Italy made it exceptionally difficult to transport such items overland. On the other hand most siege machines were easy to dismantle and to move around if suitable transport was available. For example it took 12 carts 10 days to carry military machines from London to the siege of Bytham in 1221, and their average of 10 miles per day was quite impressive.

The administrative effort of assembling and organising siege weaponry is nowhere better illustrated than in the records of the siege of Bedford castle by King Henry III in 1224.[1] Even after Bedford Castle surrendered, the King's clerks still had work to do, listing the costs involved: 'For carriage of mangonels and the said ropes for mangonels to Bedford … £1 5s. 10d.' And on 19 August, shortly after the surrender: 'The King to the Sheriff of Bedfordshire greeting. We order that you cause Our petraries and mangonels and belfry [movable siege tower], which on Our departure from Bedford We left behind us, to be disjointed and carried to Northampton, and delivered to the Sheriff of Northamptonshire … '

It was generally easier to transport siege machinery by sea or river, though this was not necessarily quicker. For the English siege of Berwick in 1333, for example, three ships named *Gracedieu*, *Jonete* and *Nicholas* carried the great mangonels from Hull to Berwick, plus 691 carefully rounded stone balls for use as ammunition.[2]

1 G.H. Fowler, 'Munitions in 1224', Publications of the Bedfordshire Historical Records Society, V (1920), pp 117–32.
2 R. Nicholson, 'The Siege of Berwick, 1333', The Scottish Historical Review, XL (1961), p. 27.

The use of medieval siege machines was more sophisticated than is generally realised and they seem to have been brought into operation in much the same sequence as described in Byzantine or Islamic sources. A siege would either start with a sudden attempt to catch the garrison unprepared or with a blockade. Siege machines would then be assembled or built, the smaller devices opening the attack while larger machines were still being constructed. Meanwhile the defenders would usually try to destroy these machines, commonly by setting them on fire. Being made of timber and normally set up close to the enemy's defences, siege engines were extremely vulnerable to fire. The short range of even the most powerful stone-throwing machines made them similarly vulnerable.

Stone-throwing engines based upon the beam-sling principle steadily increased in complexity until the widespread adoption of gunpowder firearms. Until then the arms race between stone-throwing machines and fortifications was evenly balanced. Whereas early forms of man-powered beam-sling mangonel were primarily anti-personnel weapons to clear defenders from a wall or to demolish the relatively flimsy crenellations of such walls, the heavier counterweight trebuchets of the 13th and 14th centuries could damage all but the strongest fortifications.

Nevertheless, mining was the usual method of bringing down a wall or tower. Furthermore missile-throwing machines also had an important psychological impact, dropping substantial rocks upon those inside fortifications, smashing houses and terrorising the inhabitants of a city as well as hurling filth, dead animals, the heads of slain enemies and occasionally the corpses of prisoners.

THE BACKGROUND

It has often been assumed that the collapse of the western half of the Roman Empire meant that the technological knowledge of the Classical World had little influence on siege warfare in the so-called Dark Ages. In reality it seems that it was not the knowledge which disappeared, but the socio-economic structure which enabled rulers to make use of sophisticated military technology. Without the wealth and political authority of Roman emperors, the kings of early medieval Europe lacked the capability of maintaining siege trains and a corps of skilled, literate engineers. A great deal of knowledge survived, if only in an archaic and theoretical form. Furthermore, many early medieval military leaders must have been aware of the highly effective siege technologies of contemporary armies in the Byzantine and Islamic worlds. Nevertheless, much of the military knowledge that survived from Roman times was old-fashioned when compared with the astonishing equipment available to those Byzantine and Islamic commanders.

Late Roman military technology had included a variety of forms of stone- or bolt-throwing machines based upon the torsion principle of stored energy, and was also aware of the crossbow as a means of shooting a missile. But all such machines were primarily designed to throw missiles with a roughly flat trajectory, usually as anti-personnel weapons rather than to damage enemy fortifications, though they also proved effective in delivering incendiary materials against an enemy's wooden

Large stone-throwing machines were often sited to defend the approaches to a gate. One appears in the background on a wall-painting of the early 14th-century Sienese commander Guidoriccio da Fogliano by Simone Martini. Note that the beam-sling is constructed of several lengths of timber lashed together with rope bindings. (In situ Palazzo Pubblico, Siena)

The City Charter of Carlisle, dated 1316, includes a little-known drawing of the unsuccessful Scottish siege of Carlisle in 1315. Here the Scots have a counterweight trebuchet which one operator is attempting to loose with a mallet (left). A second operator has been transfixed, probably by an arrow shot by the English great crossbow mounted on the city wall (centre). (Cumbria Records Office, Carlisle)

siege engines. Ironically, perhaps, the basic concept of the beam-sling as a means of throwing something bulkier was also known to the Romans in the form of the fustibale or staff-sling, but this was not developed into a larger siege weapon.

Very Late Roman technical treatises such as the Epitome of Military Science by Vegetius, and the anonymous De Rebus Bellicis, continued to be copied and read, though the degree of influence these texts had remains very unclear. Late Roman machines that survived into the early medieval period and beyond included the onager. This was a 4th-century AD simplified single-armed replacement of the ancient two-armed stone-throwing machines. Like those earlier devices, the onager and its presumed smaller cousin the scorpio, used the stored torsion power of twisted ropes of animal tendons or horsehair. The only serious disadvantage of the onager, compared with earlier two-armed torsion machines, was the difficulty of changing its line of fire.

Another Late Roman military technological development was a trend away from the torsion to the tension method of storing energy. In other words using a flexible bow rather than twisted skeins of fibre. Weapons based upon the crossbow principle seem to have been used in the defence of Late Roman frontier fortifications during the 4th and 5th centuries, some large enough to be mounted on frames while others were spanned by a windlass or other mechanism. It has even been suggested that the rarely mentioned Late Roman 'Thunderbolt' ballista was a crossbow that incorporated a steel bow. The Romans had the technology for such a remarkable weapon, but the circumstances of their collapsing Empire must have rendered this 'Thunderbolt' ballista extremely rare.[3]

There can be little doubt that Roman military technology survived the fall of the western half of the Empire. Regions where Roman-Latin culture remained relatively unaffected by Germanic conquest were often the same regions where sophisticated siege technology re-emerged in the 6th and 7th centuries, implying that such knowledge had never been lost. Nor were these survivals all clustered around the Roman Mediterranean heartlands, since some evidence points to comparable survivals in the Celtic west and north of Britain. Might the 6th-century Welsh poet Taliesin have been more than merely poetic when, in his verses On the

3 P.E. Chevedden, 'Artillery in Late Antiquity: Prelude to the Middle Ages', in I.A. Corfis & M. Wolfe (eds), *The Medieval City under Siege* (Woodbridge 1995), pp 156–60.

Death of Uthyr Pendragon, he wrote: 'I have broken a hundred fortresses'?

On the European mainland the defence of the Late Roman frontiers in south-western Germany was often done by assimilated German settlers, and the Germanic Goth rulers of early 6th-century Italy clearly made use of Late Roman siege technology. The idea that such devices could only have been used and maintained by ex-Roman soldiers or their immediate descendants implies that the Germanic 'barbarians' were unwilling and incapable of learning. Meanwhile in several parts of France there is strong evidence that local levies continued to play a major military role and that they remained skilled in siege warfare. Furthermore, the fact that siege warfare was more sophisticated, better organized and better equipped in southern than in northern France supports the idea that Late Roman siege technology survived more strongly in the most Romanized regions.

Another channel through which more modern siege technology reached early medieval western Europe was, of course, from the Byzantine Empire itself. King Charles the Bald of France probably recruited Byzantine engineers to make 'new machines' during the Viking siege of Angers in 873 and these machines are likely to have been of the new beam-sling form rather than a reintroduction of now outdated Roman torsion-powered artillery. The beam-sling mangonel does seem to have reached France by the 10th century, either from Byzantium, or from a variety of sources including Islamic Spain and the Asiatic Avars in central Europe. Similarly those Byzantine warships that helped Hugh of Arles, the King of Italy, attack an Arab-Islamic garrison in Fraxinetum in the 10th century brought with them another new form of siege weapon – Greek Fire – which the Romans never knew.

Equally as important as the survival of Late Roman siege technology was the influence of the early medieval Islamic world. Not only was Islamic civilization the most technologically minded the world had yet seen, but its wide-ranging trade contacts made it a vital channel for military ideas, not only those developed by Islamic armies themselves but also those from India and China. Since Muslim soldiers fought alongside as well as against those of Christian western Europe, often in circumstances where their expertise in siege warfare made them particularly valuable, they may have helped spread new ideas.

In the 12th century a more open-minded European attitude towards the mechanical arts reflected contact with the Arab-Islamic world via Spain, Sicily, the Crusades and trade contacts in general.

It would have a profound impact on the use of technology to improve medieval European industry, agriculture, architecture – and siege warfare. Indeed, from the 12th century onwards, western Europeans were living in a 'mechanism-minded world' which found the assimilation of new technologies much easier than had been the case even in

Early forms of man-powered stone-throwing mangonel were used in defence of fortified places. The simple form shown in this copy of Beatus' Commentaries on the Apocalypse, made in Gerona around 1100, is identical to the Arab lu'ab, from which it probably derived. (Ms. J. II.j, f.190r, Bib. Nazionale, Turin)

ancient Greece and Rome. By the mid-12th century there were clear similarities between siege machines used in northern Italy and those used by the Crusader States, Syria and Egypt. Late 12th- and 13th-century references to Turkish mangonels in France, England and elsewhere surely indicate that some such devices had been adopted from Muslim peoples. When an engineer, helping defend the French castle of Beaucaire in 1216, took a pot and filled it with alquitran to destroy the besiegers' chatte or armoured roof the evidence of

Walter de Milemete's treatise De Notabilibus, Sapientiis et Prudentiis Regum showed siege machines ranging from devices that were in common use to fanciful ideas that are unlikely to have been put into practice. The author is believed to have got some of the latter from ancient texts or lost non-European sources. A: Kite to drop incendiary bombs on an enemy town. B: Large frame-mounted crossbow spanned with a winch and capstan. C: Grossly misunderstood representation of a torsion-powered catapult comparable to the Roman onager or Islamic ziyar. D: Multi-armed device to hurl containers of Greek Fire, powered by a weight like a church clock. E: Movable siege tower incorporating an assault bridge. F: Large frame-mounted siege-crossbow spanned with threaded screw and capstan. G: Assault on a castle by soldiers using scaling ladders while a man with a mallet drives in stakes to secure the base of one ladder. (Ms. 92, Christ Church College Library, Oxford, England)

an exchange of ideas becomes undeniable since alquitran comes from the Arabic word al-qidr meaning a large fire-grenade. The influence of Islamic siege technology and war-machines was, of course, even more obvious in Spain and Portugal where military terminology remained strongly influenced by Arabic until the late 13th and 14th centuries.

THROWING MACHINES

Torsion-powered

The two-armed torsion-powered siege engines favoured by the Romans demanded great skill to make, maintain and use. Furthermore the twisted sinews which were their source of power had a limited useful lifespan. The single-armed torsion-powered onager was simpler, though it similarly relied upon twisted skeins of sinew. Such factors meant that the single-armed onager, or ballista as it was generally known in medieval Europe, was used in only limited numbers following the fall of the Roman Empire. Furthermore the onager-ballista was soon superceded by beam-sling stone-throwers. It is also worth noting that medieval European torsion-powered engines used horse or cattle hair for the twisted fasces which provided their power, rather than the animal tendons and ligaments preferred by Greeks and Romans. This was probably for economic reasons, since the use of hair did not necessitate killing the animal. During early Carolingian campaigns ballistas or balistas usually seem to have been constructed at the site of a siege, though it is logical to assume that metallic parts and the animal hair fasces would have been brought in the siege train.

Many scholars maintain that the mangonel was, in fact, the medieval form of the Late Roman torsion-powered onager. This results from medieval chroniclers and poets using military terminology in a looser manner than engineers are likely to have done. For example, when Otto of Freising calls the mangonel a 'type of ballista' he probably meant that both the ballista and the beam-sling mangonel threw stones. During the 9th century, references to ballistae become more frequent and even King Alfred of Wessex's translation of Orosius mentions a palistar, though there is no evidence that such a weapon was actually used in Anglo-Saxon England. In 1210 the defenders of the French castle of Termes had ballistae with sufficient range to pick off individual besiegers as they stood in the doors of their tents and they were mentioned in government documents dealing with the siege of Bedford in 1224: (27 June) 'The King to the Sheriffs of London greeting. We command you without delay to cause Hugh de Nevill to have good waggons for ten balistae and ten targets [shields] to be conveyed to Us at Bedford. That you also cause the same Hugh to have good filum [twine] to make ropes for Our balistae, up to the amount of

'The Siege of Naples' in Peter of Eboli's Chronicle illustrates simple man-powered mangonels being used in both attack and defence. The manuscript was made in Sicily or southern Italy in the early 13th century. (Ms. Cod. 120/II, f. 15a, Burgerbibliothek, Bern)

'The Siege of Antioch' in William of Tyre's History of Outremer, made in Acre shortly before the Crusader city fell in the late 13th century. This man-powered mangonel is of a type sometimes interpreted as a half-way form combining both a fixed counterweight and a team of rope-pullers. (Ms. 828, f.33r, Bib. Munic. Lyons)

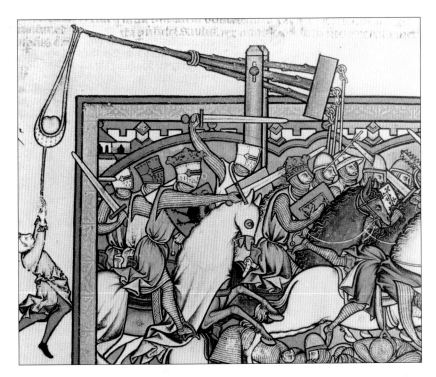

The beam-sling of the man-powered mangonel in this illustration of 'Saul's army destroying Nahash' in the mid-13th-century French Maciejowski Bible is made of roughly trimmed boughs or tree-trunks lashed together with rope. Reinforcing stitches can also be seen in the sling itself. (f. 23v, Pierpont Morgan Library, New York)

half a mark [a large value coin] …'

Within the Iberian peninsula such weapons were reintroduced by the Muslim Arabs rather than having survived since Roman times. In fact the Spanish term algarrada or algarada came from the Arabic term al-'arradah, which was, perhaps, an improved Islamic form of the ancient onager. Instead of declining in the 13th century, this algarrada increased in popularity, perhaps indicating that, like the 'arradah, it had been improved since Roman times.

Other terms might also have referred to torsion-powered siege engines. For example the chable, and other variations on this name, might have been such a weapon. It appears in the mid- to late 11th-century French Chanson de Roland as the chadable, and as a calabre in the late 12th-century La Geste de Loherin. This French word also meant a sort of folding door, which seems to suggest that it was used descriptively for a siege machine. On the other hand, at the French siege of English-held Château Gaillard in 1203–04 the French caable or Latin cabulus was also called a magna petraria and was used against the gate of the second enceinte or courtyard, which suggests that it was a large beam-sling engine rather than one based upon torsion-power. In 1282 King Charles of Naples' military stores included an engine called a capre, which may have been another variation on the basic term, as might a late 13th- or early 14th-century Spanish siege machine called a colafre.

German Crusaders attacking the fortified Estonian town of Tartu in 1224 used paterells to shoot glowing iron or ceramic fire-pots. The word probably came from patera meaning a dish or cup, which suggests a single-armed ballista-type machine, rather than a mangonel with a leather sling. On the other hand, the paterell was simple enough for Estonian tribesmen to build their own as soon as they made peace with Danish Crusaders. Within Germany itself variations on another word were also used: selbschoss, seilbscoz and seilgeschütze, which indicate a 'cord' or 'cord-powered' device comparable to the medieval Latin-based term ballista or balistarius.

The Beam-sling Mangonel

Although the staff-sling was known to the Romans, it was the Chinese who thought of mounting a larger staff-sling on a fixed pole or a wooden frame, thus inventing a highly effective means of throwing larger rocks.

Meanwhile the simple staff-sling continued to be used in early medieval Europe. In Anglo-Saxon England it was known as the staef-lidere and the fact that it was translated as ballista in Old English–Latin word lists suggests that it was used in siege warfare. The fundibularii or 'slingers' who defended Iberian towns in the 12th and 13th centuries probably used the staff-slings that appear in Iberian pictorial sources. The same was probably true of those Sicilian slingers who defended Messina against King Richard of England in the late 12th century. At the same time French epic poems and chronicles similarly mentioned slings being used in siege warfare while the 13th-century northern Italian siege warfare cazafrustum was certainly a staff-sling.

The man-powered beam-sling mangonel was invented in China between the 5th and 3rd centuries BC, reaching the Middle East by at least the 7th century AD. The smallest form could be operated by a single man pulling a single rope, but the most common types were powered by teams of from 20 to over 100 men or women, usually two per rope. In smaller mangonels the fulcrum at the top of the supporting frame was usually positioned so that five or six times as much of the beam-sling was to the rear, with the sling and missile, as was to the front with the pulling ropes. In larger mangonels the ratio was around two or three to one. Modern experiments indicate that such engines could throw projectiles weighing up to 60 kg and achieve a range of 85–133 metres.

Quite how they reached Europe is still a matter of debate, nor are mangonels likely to have arrived solely from one source. Perhaps they were introduced by the Avars in the 6th century. These Avars certainly possessed advanced arms, armour and military organisation, and had been driven from the northern frontiers of China only a few decades earlier. The first specific description of beam-sling machines in

The mid-13th-century Italian Annales de Genes includes a number of important sketches of early counterweight trebuchets, including a frame that has yet to have its beam-sling (a), as well as large (c) and small (b) forms of man-powered mangonels. (Ms. Lat. 10136, ff. 107r, 141v-142r, Bib. Nat., Paris)

a

b

c

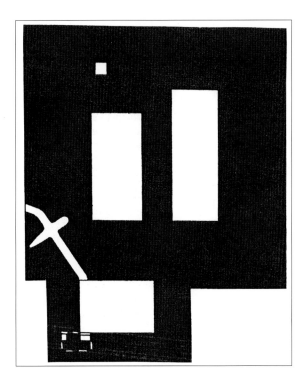

A plan of Bungay Castle, England, as it was in the 12th century. During a siege of the castle by King Henry II a mine was driven beneath the south-western angle of the keep to make the structure collapse. A transverse gallery was also excavated before the owner of the castle paid a large ransom to save his castle.

Europe comes from the writings of the Byzantine Greek Archbishop John of Thessaloniki (see New Vanguard: *Medieval Siege Engines (2)*), who described the stone-throwing engines used by an Avar–Slav army in AD 597. Another clear reference to a manganum is in the biography of King Louis the Pious, but unfortunately this merely lists the manganum alongside other siege equipment used against Islamic Tortosa in Spain in 808–09. By that time, of course, the Muslim Arabs were themselves making considerable use of what they called the manjaniq. Other evidence hints at the beam-sling siege-machine being localised in Aquitaine and the Pyrenean frontier region, which would suggest that the manganum reached France from the western Islamic lands.

By the late 9th century the mangonel was more widespread, apparently being used in defence of Paris against Viking attack in 885–86. Here, according to Abbo of Saint-Germain:

'The Franks prepared some heavy pieces of wood each with an iron tooth at the end, so as to damage the Danish [siege] machines more quickly. With coupled beams of the same length they built what are commonly called mangonels, machines for throwing vast stones … '

The first Latin source to include the comparable term petraria was the Chronicon Salernitatum, written by Paul the Deacon around 980. This word is assumed to derive from the Byzantine Greek petrare, which was almost certainly a man-powered beam-sling engine, known in the 7th century. Whether the fact that the term petrary came to refer to a larger machine than the mangonel reflected some general difference between the Byzantine petrare and the Arab-Islamic manjaniq is, however, unknown.

By the late 11th century large rock-throwing siege machines were being used by Christian armies in Spain, these almost certainly being identical to the Andalusian-Arab manjaniqs. The First Crusaders may have used small beam-sling machines inside Antioch in 1098, but the term mangonele did not appear in French written sources until the late 12th century. Other machines called patrariae, or variations of this word, were used in Anglo-Norman England and France from the mid-12th century. King Philip Augustus of France took three, or at least the technical parts of three, such petrariae with him on the Third Crusade, while in England petraries were mentioned during the sieges of Marlborough and Nottingham in 1194.

There is sufficient evidence to suggest that these words did have a relatively precise meaning amongst the military engineers who built and operated them. For example when the two appeared together, the perrière, patraria or petrary usually referred to a beam-sling siege machine that was larger than the mangonel. Most written sources also indicate that the petrary was used to damage fortifications, which suggests a substantial missile. During Philip Augustus' siege of Boves it took four men to carry each stone for the pierrières or

13

petraries.[4] In later years, however, petraries were sometimes described as 'lesser machines', but this was probably in comparison with the much more powerful counterweight trebuchet (see below).

The term mangonel only became widespread in Europe in the 13th century. In Spain they were more commonly called almanganiqs or alma-jenechs, from the Arabic term, though the words manguanels or manganillas do appear. Furthermore, beam-sling engines also seem to have been used in larger number within the Iberian peninsula, again almost certainly reflecting Arab-Islamic influence. For more detailed information we have to wait until 1293, when a comprehensive inventory of the arsenal at Carcassonne was drawn up for the new garrison commander. This stated that the available siege equipment included:

'It. II pousserios ferri as mangonnellos. (2 levers for mangonels)

It. III furcas de mangonellis. (3 axles for mangonels)

It. VI turnos pro ingeniis et mangonellis. (6 winches for engines and mangonels)

It. XII claves ad virgas ingeniorum. (12 triggers for axles for engines)

It. sex cavillas ferri quadratus al ponendum in bigues.' (six squared iron pegs for the rear of the bases of mangonels)

The term ingenium referred to all siege engines. A mangonel and a trebuchet both included a virga or horizontal arm or beam-sling, and a bigua base or frame. The mangonel emerges as the weaker machine whose construction and use involved a huge quantity of ropes of various sizes.[5] A few years later, in the 14th-century Dalmatian port-city of Dubrovnik, mangona were again described as 'small machines'.

Although the western European mangonel was not recorded in as many versions as was the Arab-Islamic manjaniq, it did have one interesting variation. This was known as the Turkish mangonel, which appears in the biography of King Philip Augustus of France by Guillaume

In 1335 Guido da Vigevano wrote a remarkable engineering treatise, the Texaurus, which mixes the practical with the fanciful. Most of the machines are based upon existing technology, though sometimes taken to impractical extremes. A: Elevating platform to enable troops to attack an enemy in a high position. B: Multiple scaling ladder incorporating an assault bridge. C: Siege tower with a platform raised and lowered by ropes. D: Fortified tower on wheels. (Ms. Lat. 11015, Bibliothèque Nationale, Paris, France)

4 E. Robert, 'Guerre et fortification dans la Philippide de Guillaume le Breton: approches archéologiques', in G. De Boe & F. Verhaeghe (eds), Military Studies in Medieval Europe – Papers of the 'Medieval Europe Brugge 1997' Conference, Volume 11 (Zellik 1997), p 16.

5 G.J. Mot, 'L'arsenal et le parc de matériel à la Cité de Carcassonne en 1298', Annales du Midi, LXVIII (1956), pp 412–14.

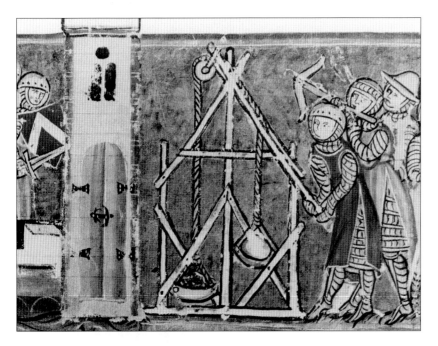

Siege scene in Willehalm by Wolfram von Eschenbach, German c.1320. The machine in this illustration seems to defy interpretation, yet its similarity to the base-frame of a trebuchet might indicate that the artist was working from a technical manual which he did not understand. (Ms. Pal. Germ. 848, f.81v, Universitätsbibliothek, Heidelberg)

de Breton, as 'mangonellus, Turcorum more, minora … ', suggesting that this Turkish form again came in large and small versions. It was called the manganell turquès in early to mid-13th-century Spain. In France there was also a 'Turkish' form of the petrary.

Other terms for apparent beam-sling siege engines are more difficult to define. For example the 'Balearic' fundae slings used by Crusaders against Islamic Lisbon in the mid-12th century were too fast in operation to be versions of the counterweight trebuchet. Perhaps the chronicler was showing off his knowledge of the Balearic slingers in Roman armies, or perhaps they were small, fast-shooting, man-powered mangonels hurling relatively light rocks, of the type known in the Islamic world – including the Balearic Islands – as the lu'ab.

The frondevola of late 12th-century southern France and the fonevol of early 13th-century Aragon appear to be very light forms of almajanech or mangonel, easily transported by sea and used to defend a field fortification. The arnalda that destroyed an Islamic trebuchet during the Aragonese conquest of Majorca was clearly a stone-throwing machine, while the tormenta seems to have been an unspecified smaller form of mangonel.

The way these man-powered siege engines were used can shed light on their power and effectiveness. They were often, if not almost always, used in batteries of several machines and at the French siege of Château Gaillard they were placed ahead of the French positions, presumably because of their limited range. During the siege of Lisbon in 1147 teams of 100 English Crusaders operated two machines in shifts, managing to throw no fewer than 5,000 rocks in 10 hours – roughly one every seven seconds. During a siege of Rouen in 1174 batteries of stone-throwers were operated by men working in eight-hour shifts. Even if the missiles were small, the moral impact of such a sustained barrage must have been considerable and in 1145 the brand new castle of Farington in England surrendered following such a prolonged bombardment, without the besiegers needing to make a general assault. A poem called Ercan li Rozier by the French troubadour Bernat Arnaut de Moncuc, written around 1212, suggests that even man-powered mangonels could damage a stone fortification:

'Be m plazo l'arquier
Pres la barbarcana,
Cant trazo l peirier

E l mur dezanvana
E per mant verdier
Creis la ost e gensa.'

(I take pleasure in the archers near the loopholes when the stone-throwing machines shoot and the wall loses its parapet, and when the army increases in numbers and forms ordered ranks in many an orchard).[6]

These machines did not merely throw whatever rocks were available. To maintain accuracy the missiles had to be of a standardised weight and shape, so masons were vital members of the siege train. They not only shaped the rocks but selected suitable stone. Timber gates were a natural target and this tactic was mentioned in many verses and chronicles.

Another scene in Willehalm by Wolfram von Eschenbach shows an attack on a coastal or riverside fortification by 'King Tybalt's galley'. Again the machine in this illustration seems to defy interpretation, though it may be intended to show some sort of dropping device rather than a trebuchet. (Ms. Pal. Germ. 848, f.33v, Universitätsbibliothek, Heidelberg)

Sometimes this was attempted from close range while at other times it was possible for larger machines to shoot at an inner gate, apparently even before the outer wall and gates had fallen.

Defending forces made just as much use of beam-sling engines as did besiegers and they were accurate enough to pick off enemy leaders, as when a woman-powered mangonel in Toulouse killed Gui de Montfort.

However it was more common for defending machines to target the attackers' machines, including siege towers. Man-powered mangonels were relatively small, so it was common for them to be erected on top of towers and gates. Height clearly gave an advantage to a stone-throwing machine. For example the German Emperor Barbarossa mounted a mangonel on top of a captured Roman arch during his siege of Milan in 1158, but it was destroyed by Milanese counter-battery fire. The mangonels mounted on the numerous family-owned torri or tall slender towers which were a feature of 12th-to 14th-century Italian cities would have enjoyed an even greater height advantage. They would shoot at each other, tower to tower, or would bombard street barricades below during the family feuds that tore many Italian cities apart.

Counter-battery work against enemy stone-throwers often seems to have been the major task for mangonels and petraries. During the siege of Tortona in Italy in 1155 there was a specific reference to one stone-throwing engine being damaged by an enemy machine, though it was repaired and returned to action. Wooden siege towers were similarly vulnerable and the fate of one provides perhaps the best descriptions of

6 F.M. Chambers, 'Three Troubadour Poems with Historical Overtones', *Speculum*, LIV (1979), pp 48–50.

the effectiveness of woman-powered mangonels (see Plate C). Attempts were, of course, made to mount small mangonels on the top of siege towers. According to Orderic Vitalis, Robert de Bellême constructed 'machines which were wheeled against the enemy's castle, hurling great stones at the fortress and its garrison' during the siege of Bréval in 1092. A less successful armed tower had been used against Durazzo (now Durrës in Albania) by the Italo-Norman leader Robert Guiscard in 1081.

It was sometimes even possible for mangonels to hit moving targets, as the Crusaders did during their siege of Damietta in 1249. Here five or six mangonels shot rocks and pots of quicklime at Islamic galleys in the River Nile, sinking three of them. During a naval siege of Barcelona in 1359 the defenders sited their siege machines along the beach to stop enemy ships coming ashore. There are also a few references to the use of mangonels or petraries at sea though only, it seems, in the relatively calm conditions of the Mediterranean and usually against static targets such as enemy harbours.

Various materials were needed to make a beam-sling engine, in addition to large baulks of timber. Once again records of the siege of Bedford in 1224 provide remarkable details. Here King Henry III's clerks sent numerous letters to various officials, demanding that they provide materials: (20 June) 'The King to the Sheriffs of London greeting. We command you that, as you love us, with all speed that you can, you send to Us to Bedford two or three carts loads of ropes, and 20 slings for mangonells and petraries,' (24 June) 'The King to the Bailiffs of Northampton greeting. We command you without delay to send to Us at Bedford under safe guard ten white oxen or horse hides, or ten or twelve tanned hides, to make slings for petraries and mangonells.' Many other

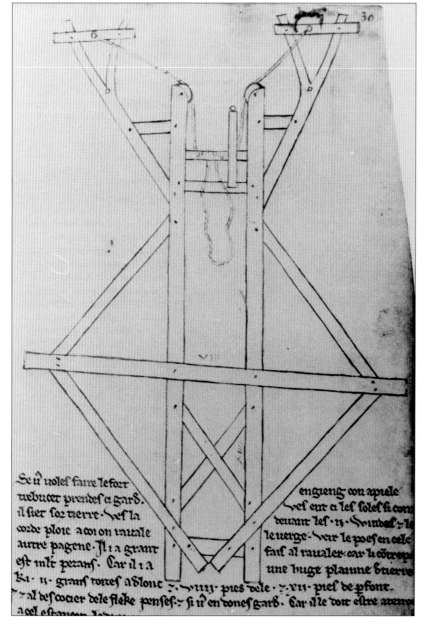

Drawing of the base of a trebuchet in the Sketch Book of Villard de Honnecourt, c.1250. (Ms. 19093, f. C.LIX, Bib. Nat., Paris)

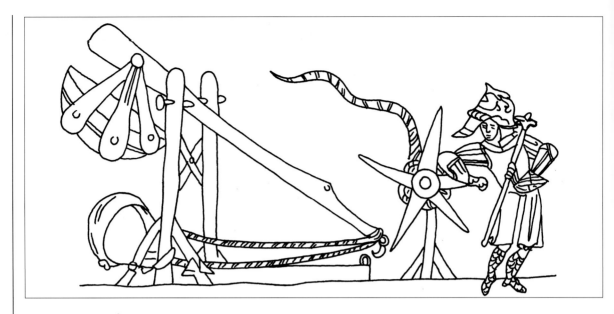

letters demanded ropes, which were required in large numbers. (25 June) 'The King to the Sheriff of Dorset greeting. We order you, as soon as these letters have been seen, to buy ten pounds worth of ropes and without delay to cart them to Us at Bedford, for the use of Our mangonells and Our Petraries.' Ox-hides to make slings were one of the most expensive items in the list of costs, which also included money for 'Four tools for sewing slings'.

There were no references to the metallic parts of such siege machines and these were presumably brought from the King's own arsenal in the Royal Wardrobe. Ammunition and other items were a different matter. (30 June) 'The King to the Sheriff of Bedfordshire greeting. We order you without delay to cause to come to Us at Bedford at Our charges all the quarriers and stone-cutters in your jurisdiction, with levers, sledges, mallets, wedges, and other necessary tools, to work stones for mangonells and petraries.' On 25 July a letter to the Bailiffs of Northampton demanded 'twenty sheaves of good steel and a load of good Gloucester iron, and six loads of planks, and twelve white hides and eight tanned hides'.[7]

In England the hide or leather slings on mangonels and petraries were themselves called baudres. English records also show that ropes for petraries and mangonels were sent to Portsmouth where a war-fleet was assembling, while in the late 13th century most of the ropes for the siege machines constructed in the Tower of London were themselves made, not surprisingly, in the great seaport of Bristol. Less is known about the small metallic pieces in such siege machines, though the documentary evidence does indicate that they involved copper and tin. This was probably to make bronze elements such as axles.

The Counterweight Trebuchet
The counterweight trebuchet was invented in the eastern Mediterranean region or Middle East, during or before the first half of the 12th century

An armoured engineer operating a counterweight trebuchet in one of the most realistic illustrations in the De Notabilibus, Sapientiis et Prudentiis Regum, a treatise on military technology by Walter de Milemete around 1326. The machine is accompanied by a winch and capstan while the operator carries a long-handled hammer with a doubled claw on one side. (Ms. 92, f. 67, Christ Church College Library, Oxford, England)

7 Fowler, op. cit., pp 119–29.

(see New Vanguard *Medieval Siege Machines (2) Byzantium, the Islamic World & India*). Here and in medieval Western Europe the required timber technology was shared with non-military machines. For example, in late 13th-century England large cranes used for building projects, and the more complex siege machines, were both made in the Tower of London. It is, however, difficult to trace the spread of the trebuchet from the Middle East to Europe because European written sources were less specific in their use of terminology than were Arabic and Greek texts.

During the Emperor Barbarossa's siege of Tortona in 1155, one of the mangonels caused an upper part of the fortifications to collapse, killing three men beneath. Perhaps this exceptionally powerful mangonel was actually a new counterweight trebuchet. An unusual and perhaps early version of the term, trebuchel, also appeared in a late 12th-century French poem, the Chanson d'Ogier. The Romano family, ancestors of the warlike Ezzelino whose siege train was amongst the most effective in early 13th century Italy, were said to have had great faith in the mangano and the trabuchello in 1189. But the first specific reference to a trebuchet in a historical chronicle was in a description by Codagnellus of the siege of Castelnuovo Bocca d'Adda near Cremona in Italy in 1199.

By the early 13th century some Italian trabucchi or trebuchets appear as light, easily assembled machines which could be mounted on the tops of towers, while others were notably larger, and here it is worth noting that one of the most immediate uses of counterweight trebuchets in the Islamic world was on top of fortified towers. In Spain and Portugal the comparable term trabuquet was rare, probably because Iberian terminology was dominated by words of Arabic origin. Nevertheless, these siege machines were increasingly used and a young prince like Alfonso, the future king of Castile, could be given a toy trebuchet.

According to De Joinville, the Count d'Eu also had a model siege engine which he demonstrated on the dinner table by breaking glasses.

During the 13th century counterweight trebuchets were used in France, Germany, England and elsewhere, with several variations of the word itself appearing in written sources. Prince Louis of France brought a notably large example to England during his abortive invasion of 1216 and clear references to English trebuchets started about 10 years later. In Germany the trebuchet was still considered a 'new weapon' in 1212, when

Sometimes medieval artists without practical knowledge of trebuchets illustrated totally impractical machines. Here it seems that a late 13th-century French artist has merely added a counterweight to the ropes of an inaccurately drawn light version of the single-pole mangonel. (Private collection)

Otto IV besieged Weissenburg using 'a three-armed machine called a triboke'. By the early 14th century counterweight trebuchets had reached Dalmatia where, in Dubrovnik, they were called 'large machines' in contrast to the 'small machines', which were man-powered mangonels. Even the generally old-fashioned Scots now had a few trebuchets though, while defending Stirling against the English in 1304, the Scots only had one and its arm broke.

Various sources include detailed information about the structure of ordinary trebuchets. For example, during his siege of Toulouse, Simon de Montfort's largest trebuchet had a beam-sling whose arm was 12 metres long, with a counterweight said to be 26 tonnes, though 2.6 seems more realistic. Later trebuchets normally had counterweights of between 4.5 and 13.6 tonnes, shooting projectiles weighing 45–90 kg.

One of the most frustrating sources is a drawing by the 13th-century architect and engineer Villard de Honnecourt. It illustrates the base-frame of a trebuchet with an apparently doubled winch mechanism, but was originally one of a pair of drawings. The lost illustration showed the supporting frame and perhaps beam-sling and counterweight. Next to the surviving drawing is the commentary:

'If you wish to build the strong engine called the trebucet pay close attention. Here is the base as it rests on the ground. In front are the two windlasses and the double rope by which the pole is hauled down, as you may see on the other page. The weight which must be hauled back is very great, for the counterpoise is very heavy being a hopper full of earth. This is fully two fathoms long, eight feet wide and twelve feet deep. Remember that before the missile is discharged, it must rest on the front stanchion.'[8]

The trebuchets in the inventory of the arsenal in Carcassonne in 1293 consisted of a virga horizontal arm or perhaps axle, and a bigua or base. The counterweight was made either of lead plates, petias plumbi, or stones, petras. The beam-sling or the funde ad ingenia, consisted of an arm or brachia, and a leather 'tray' or coria; the machine being drawn back with a winch or turnus, on bearings or paalarios made of copper or iron. This winch was operated by levers or pousserios and a wheel or magnus circulus, and was secured by a trigger or claves. It wound up a cable at the end of which was a capstan which incorporated

A copy of Konrad Kyeser's Bellifortis in Göttingen includes a woodcut print of a complicated trebuchet which incorporates a massive winch system and a form of protection for the operators consisting of a timber fortification at the front of the machine. By the time this was printed, however, the trebuchet had virtually fallen out of use. (Universitätsbibliothek, f. 48r., Göttingen)

8 T. Bowie, *The Sketchbook of Villard de Honnecourt* (Bloomington 1959).

This early 13th-century French picture of Crusader siege machines hurling enemy heads into Nicea shows what might be a largely misunderstood early form of the counterweight trebuchet. There are clearly no teams of rope-pullers, while the bulging ends of the beam-slings might be an artist's attempt to indicate an early form of fixed counterweight. (Ms. Fr. 2630, f.22v, Bib. Nat., Paris)

iron or copper elements, boitas ferri in quibus pollae vertuntur, to pull the arm and its ropes, vergaturis. The machine itself was held together with pins, cavillas magnas, and ropes, chables de ligaturis.[9]

English records are less specific, though King Edward I's biggest tre-buchet at the siege of Stirling took five master carpenters and 49 others three months to build. Information from another siege in Wales in 1288–89 specified that the English used pig's grease to lubricate the axles of their trebuchet. Another particularly large trebuchet named Forester, in the arsenal of Berwick-upon-Tweed in 1298, had a massive iron 'nail' or primary axle for its beam-sling. Its counterweight was also of iron, although during various sieges in Scotland in 1304 the English stripped the lead from local churches for use as trebuchet counterweights.

A few decades later a Flemish siege engineer named John Crabbe directed the English bombardment of Scottish-held Berwick. He felled 40 oak trees and 'fashioned two geat rods' for the engines – presumably meaning their beam-slings – then hired 24 oxen to haul the timber to Cowick in Yorkshire where the machines were assembled. This necessitated the conscription of carpenters, sawyers, smiths and ropers, plus a band of 37 stone masons and six quarrymen to make hundreds of stone missiles.[10]

Although several variations on the basic trebuchet are mentioned in medieval sources, most should be treated with caution. For example the tumerel mentioned by Philippe Mousket around 1260 is said to be a form of trebuchet, but as the word also meant a deadfall trap it was probably a descriptive or poetic term.

The biffa and variations on this word are similarly problematical. Some have suggested that it was a half-way version between the man-powered mangonel and the counterweight trebuchet. Such machines do seem to appear in highly stylized medieval European manuscript illustrations and it is possible that such an idea was attempted during the development of the trebuchet. It is also possible that the biffa was merely the standard trebuchet in which the counterweight was

9 Mot, op. cit., p 414.
10 Nicholson, op. cit., p 27.

attached to a second axle and was thus able to swivel around the short end of the beam-sling. On the other hand a counterweight fixed directly to the end of the beam-sling would be far less efficient than one mounted on an axle. Perhaps a second movable counter-weight might have been added to the beam-sling as a means of altering the machine's range. Evidence for this is, however, dubious and even the clear ref-erence to such trebuchets in Egidio Colonna's Reg-imine Principum, written around 1280, may be fanciful. Of Colonna's four types of trebuchet – one of which is in fact a man-powered mangonel or perrière – the second with a fixed counterweight was the most accurate, the third or biffa with a swivelling or movable counterweight had greater range, while a fourth called a tripantum sup-posedly combined both a fixed and a swinging counterweight.[11]

The illustration of a counterweight trebuchet in the early 14th-century Franco-Flemish Roman du Saint Graal, though out of scale to the figures, is remarkably accurate. The base, supporting frame, beam-sling, counterweight and even a rope to the trigger are all very realistic. (Ms. Add. 10292, f. 81v, British Library, London)

The fact that various types of siege machine were given the names of powerful animals has, of course, been widely noted. The name biffa, for example, may have come from the vernacular Italian word for a female buffalo. It may equally, and perhaps more probably, echo the name given to one Arab-Islamic trebuchet: namely the 'Black Bull' or kara bughawiyyah type of manjaniq which had been modified to hurl larger missiles. The biffa was, however, a real weapon, having been used by the people of Viterbo when besieged by the Emperor Frederick II in 1243.

Here the defenders had 'una buffa grande e una piccola' with which they were able to strike the enemy's camp.

There are similar problems with a form of trebuchet called the bricola. One of the first references to this machine was in early 13th- century Genoa. The term evolved into the brigolo, bidda, blida, bleda and bliden when used in Spain, France, Germany and Italy. It may also be the same as the biblia recorded in Flanders and taken on Crusade by King Louis of France in the mid-13th century. It could apparently throw incendiary missiles but other evidence points to it being a light form of trebuchet with a counterweight fixed in such a manner that it was almost an integral part of the beam-sling. It might also be mounted on a cart and thus almost become a form of field artillery. One edition of the De Machinis written by Mariano Taccola in the mid-15th century even includes a detailed drawing of what is labelled as a brichola; this being a light trebuchet mounted on a single

11 D.J. Cathcart King, 'The Trebuchet and other siege engines', Château-Gaillard, IX–X (1982), p 463.

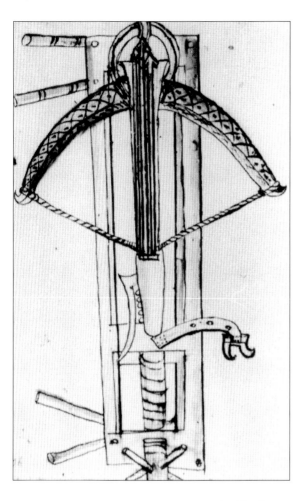

angled pole and having a forked beam-sling with two separate swivelled counterweights.

Other even more obscure machines were a so-called trabuquet de Marsella used during a siege of Palma in Majorca early in the 13th century, and a rock-throwing martinet first mentioned in a French Glossary of 1315, but nothing else is known of these devices.

The varied effectiveness of western European counterweight siege machines is clear in many documentary sources. One eye-witness account of the Crusader siege of Acre in 1189–91 maintained that they reduced the fortifications to the height of a man. On the other hand the most advanced siege machines available to Archbishop Konrad during his siege of Cologne in 1252 only succeeded in damaging one house. Elsewhere these trebuchets had a reputation of being terrifyingly accurate. The Chanson de la Croisade Albigenoise, describing the siege of Castelnaudry in September 1211, stated:

'The besiegers set up their trebuchet on a road but all around they could only find stones which would have fragmented under the impact of shooting. In the end they found three which they brought from a good league away. With their first shot they knocked down a tower. With their next, in everyone's sight, they destroyed a chamber. With the third shot the stone they loosed disintegrated, but not before causing great injury to those who

Great crossbows are mentioned more often than they are illustrated. The picture shown here comes from one of Mariano Taccola's treatises, De Ingeneis, and shows a great crossbow spanned by a screw mechanism mounted on a four-legged table. (Ms. Lat. 197, f.40r., Staatsbib., Munich)

were inside the town.'[12]

The counterweight trebuchet permitted more regular and accurate targeting than was possible with man-powered mangonels. On the other hand the dynamics of a trebuchet were so complex that it was very difficult to change the range let alone the direction of the shot. Modern reconstructions show that the heavier the stone the sooner the sling will open, but if the missile is too light, the sling will open too late and the missile will hit the ground a short distance in front of the trebuchet. Range can also be slightly increased by increasing the counterweight.

During sieges, the trebuchets were generally grouped into batteries, as had been the case with mangonels. In Italy, and perhaps to a lesser extent elsewhere, small forms of trebuchet could be used to defend field fortifications. Like the earlier mangonels, trebuchets were sometimes placed on board Italian ships to attack the walls of an enemy port. This the Pisans attempted against Genoa in 1284, though their fleet was intercepted and defeated near Meloria Island. The transportation of trebuchets was also similar to that of mangonels.

When, in 1300, the English attacked the Scottish castle of Caerlaverock some siege machines were brought by sea while another

12 K. De Vries, *Medieval Military Technology* (Peterborough, Ontario 1992), p 139.

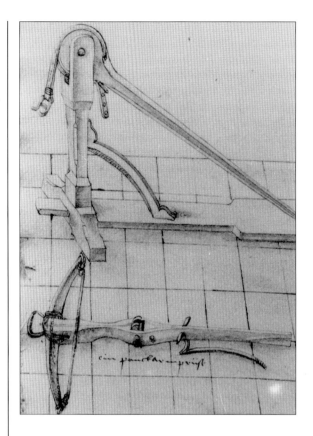
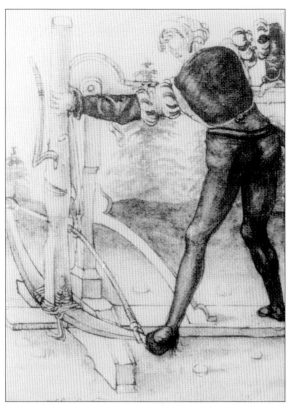

machine was hauled overland from Lochmaben. It was only a short
distance, but the move took seven men a week to complete.

Since large trebuchets created sudden stresses when shot, they were
not normally placed on walls which might be destabilised. Instead they
were placed on the roofs of larger towers and, in fact, the adoption
of large numbers of defensive trebuchets resulted in 13th-century
fortifications having more and larger projecting towers than had been
the case in the 12th century. The numbers of trebuchets in a particular
fortification would, of course, reflect the importance of the castle in
question. Writing around the year 1400 Christine de Pisan probably
reflected current opinion when she stated that such stone-throwing
machines were no longer needed to defend a place with a garrison of
fewer than 200 men, but to take a difficult fortification the besiegers
needed four engins volants and four couillars (these two groups
possibly including trebuchets) with 1,000 stones for these machines,
plus cannon with their stones.

Giant Crossbows and Espringals

A form of giant crossbow on a supporting frame is believed to have
largely replaced complex torsion-powered arrow-shooting machines
towards the end of the Late Roman period. Such giant crossbows almost
certainly incorporated bows of composite form, similar in construction
to those used by Rome's Middle Eastern archers. Evidence for their
continued use during the early medieval period is very sparse but such
weapons had reappeared in the Byzantine and Islamic worlds by the
11th century. Some evidence hints at the possibility that they were not

A: Battering ram used against St Bertrand de Comminges during a Merovingian Frankish civil war in 585

B: Siege tower used at the siege of Verdun in 985

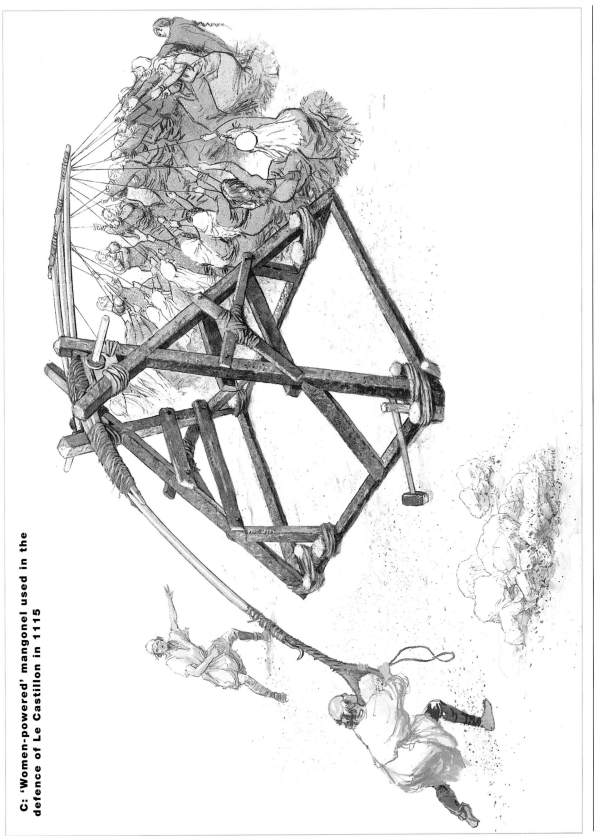

C: 'Women-powered' mangonel used in the defence of Le Castillon in 1115

D: ARMOURED ASSAULT-BRIDGE USED AT THE SIEGE OF CREMA IN JANUARY 1160

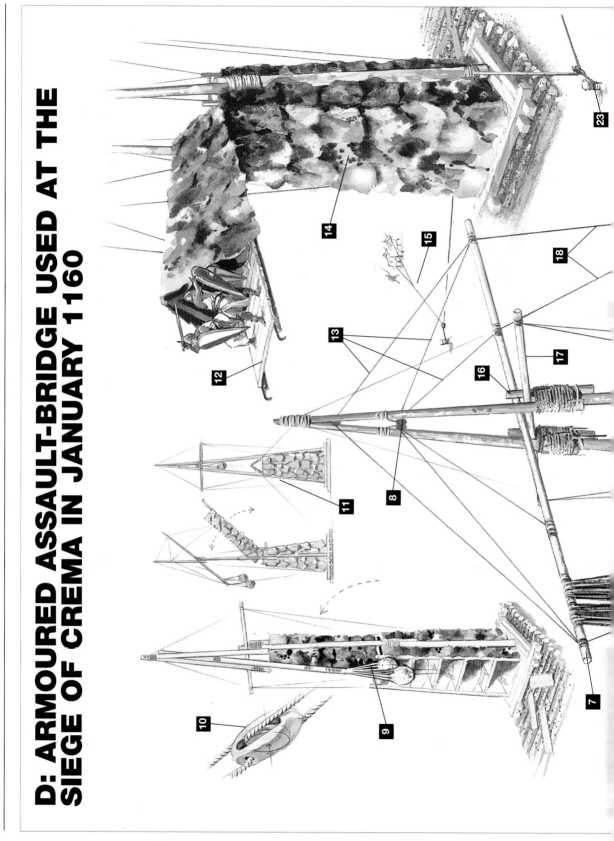

D

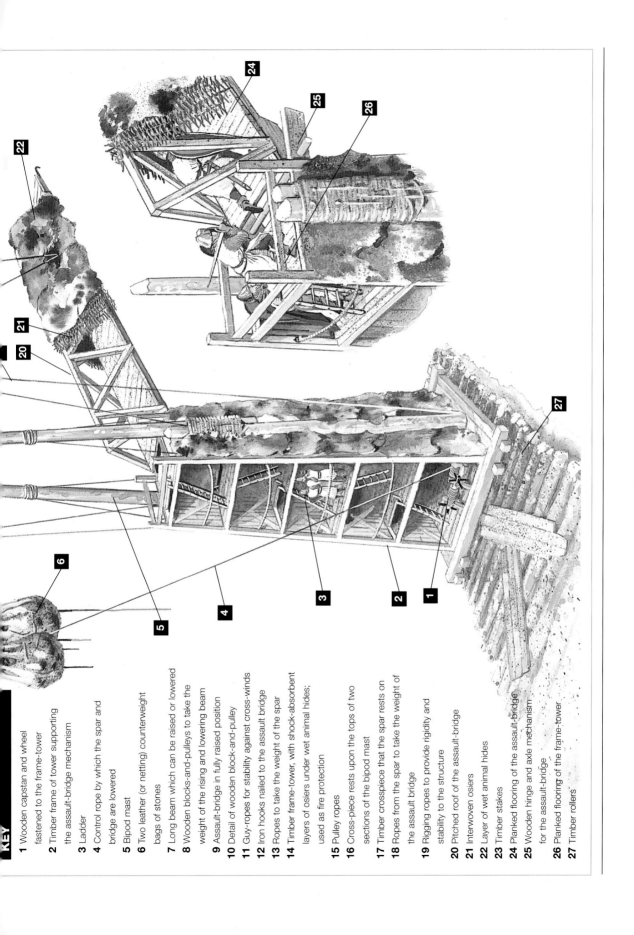

1 Wooden capstan and wheel fastened to the frame-tower
2 Timber frame of tower supporting the assault-bridge mechanism
3 Ladder
4 Control rope by which the spar and bridge are lowered
5 Bipod mast
6 Two leather (or netting) counterweight bags of stones
7 Long beam which can be raised or lowered
8 Wooden blocks-and-pulleys to take the weight of the rising and lowering beam
9 Assault-bridge in fully raised position
10 Detail of wooden block-and-pulley
11 Guy-ropes for stability against cross-winds
12 Iron hooks nailed to the assault bridge
13 Ropes to take the weight of the spar
14 Timber frame-tower, with shock-absorbent layers of osiers under wet animal hides; used as fire protection
15 Pulley ropes
16 Cross-piece rests upon the tops of two sections of the bipod mast
17 Timber crosspiece that the spar rests on
18 Ropes from the spar to take the weight of the assault bridge
19 Rigging ropes to provide rigidity and stability to the structure
20 Pitched roof of the assault-bridge
21 Interwoven osiers
22 Layer of wet animal hides
23 Timber stakes
24 Planked flooring of the assault-bridge
25 Wooden hinge and axle mechanism for the assault-bridge
26 Planked flooring of the frame-tower
27 Timber rollers

E: Crane to drop missiles used by the Scots defending Berwick against the English in 1319

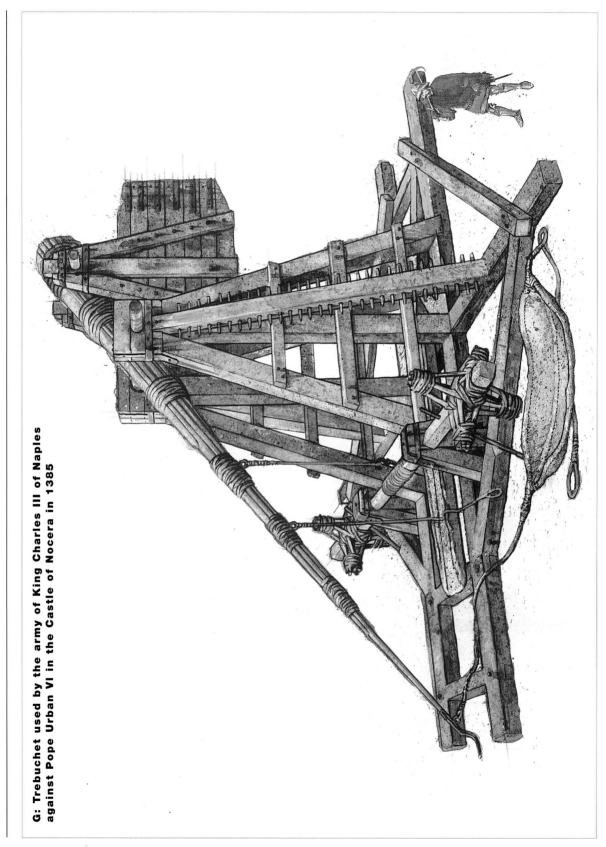

G: Trebuchet used by the army of King Charles III of Naples against Pope Urban VI in the Castle of Nocera in 1385

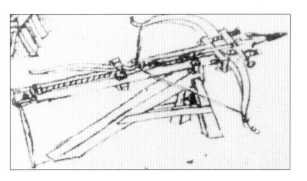

entirely abandoned in some parts of Western Europe either. For example the defenders of Paris in the late 9th century are said to have shot a great arrow which skewered several Vikings like meat on a spit. Even more frustrating is an Anglo-Saxon English riddle which seems to describe a sort of crossbow, probably a large frame-mounted type. Nevertheless, the sudden reappearance of frame-mounted arbalète á tour crossbows in western Europe must surely have reflected contact with the Byzantine and the Islamic worlds. In 1184 the Muwahhid Caliph Abu Yaqub was killed by a qaws al-lawlab while attacking the Portuguese town of Santarem. The Arab qaws al-lawlab was a heavy form of crossbow which could shoot a bolt weighing up to 2.5 kg – in other words a great crossbow – and if the isolated Portuguese possessed such weapons then surely the Spaniards must have done so, though Spanish sources do not mention the ballista de torno, as the arbalète á tour or great crossbow would be known in Iberia, until the mid-13th century.

Since medieval European crossbows came in a variety of sizes, it is not easy to specify what type rated as a siege machine. For our purposes, however, the arbalète á tour, and other variations on this term, are regarded as great crossbows. They appear in medieval art infrequently, and with their size generally exaggerated. Surviving fragments have bows from one to two metres long, and a detailed description of a great crossbow in Avignon in 1349 indicated that the bow was about 1.6 metres long. Surviving examples from the Middle East are of both composite and simple construction, but the only known great crossbow from England was made from a single stave of yew. It was found in the moat of Berkhamstead Castle, dates from around 1216 and is just under 1.25 metres long. The span was only about 20–30 cm, with a draw-weight of about 70 kg, which would have required a winch or comparable mechanism.[13]

Information about the frames on which these great crossbows were mounted is even rarer. The records of the Clos de Galées in Rouen mentions a haussepied in association with a crossbow in 1336, but it is unclear whether this was a device to help re-string the weapon or a frame on which to mount it. Records from Dubrovnik in 1361 do, however, indicate that the baliste grosse, bariste de torno, baliste a torno and magna balista could all be mounted on a pedestal called a scagno.

13 R.C. Brown, 'Observations on the Berkhamstead Bow', *Journal of the Society of Archer Antiquaries*, X (1967), pp 12–17.

Apparently the function of these weapons was to cover the approaches to such things as gates, and they usually appear to have been established in fixed positions with a limited arc of fire. Some historians maintain that they were placed in special wide embrasures but other evidence suggests that arbalètes á tour were commonly placed above towers or gates, as indicated in the Ordnance of Hughes de Cardaillac. They also seem to have been easier to transport than stone-throwing siege machines. For example in 1297 12 great crossbows, plus two windlasses and a box of spare parts were included in an arms shipment sent from London to Carlisle. A ship taking equipment for the French garrison on the recently conquered island of Guernsey in 1339 carried, amongst other weapons, three arbalètes à tour, four hauchepies and four tours, which are presumed to be mounting frames for great crossbows. But great crossbows were sometimes used to attack fortifications. Ballestas de torno certainly featured in King Fernando III's siege of Seville, while the Aragonese used them to drive Muslim defenders from the walls of the city of Palma in Majorca during the same period. At sea great crossbows were more useful than espringals (see below) because they were less vulnerable to damp; those aboard 13th-century French warships were spanned by

a

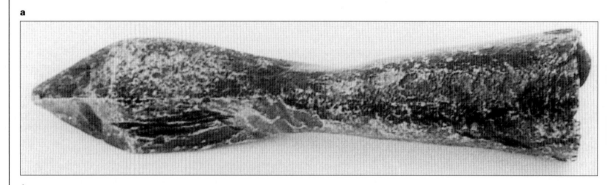

b

A – Iron bolt-head from the castle of Hasenburg in Switzerland. It weighs 171.25 gm and was probably intended for a great crossbow or an espringal. (No. 2854.4, Historisches Museum, Lucerne).
B – The point of another heavy missile from the Papal Palace in Avignon. Though heavily corroded, it weighs 105 gm and incorporates an anti-ricochet ring based upon the same principle as those used in several modern bombs and missiles. (Via Jean Liebel)

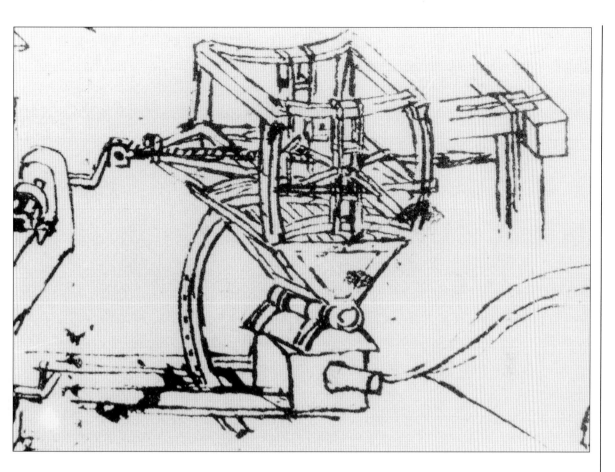

winches on a frame. The written records of leading Italian maritime republics include numerous references to variations of the great crossbow, as when Venetian regulations on ships' armaments in 1255 stated that each balista de torno vel de pesarola was to have 50 quarrels as ammunition.

The espringal fulfilled the same function as the great crossbow, but was a more complex and more powerful weapon, being an improved version of the Hellenistic-Roman torsion-powered catapulta. It consisted of a wooden frame mounted on a support and contained two separate 'bow-arms', each thrust through twisted skeins of animal hair. Down the centre of the frame was a sort of crossbow tiller or stock with a groove for a large arrow or other missile, plus a trigger and a revolving-nut release mechanism. This extremely powerful weapon was drawn or spanned mechanically, usually by a winch or screw.

There is no evidence that the Roman catapulta survived in early medieval Europe, though it almost certainly did so within the Byzantine Empire. However, the European espringal is more likely to have sprung from the medieval Islamic qaws al-ziyar or 'skein bow'. Quite when it reappeared in western Europe is unclear, but it was probably as a result of the Crusades. During the preparations for King Louis' disastrous expedition against Egypt in 1250, one of the royal scribes felt it necessary to explain what was regarded as a new weapon, calling it a previously unknown balistrarium silvestrarum vel spingardarum, wooden ballista or spingardarum.

French versions of the name, espringale or espringarde, first appear in a manuscript from Reims dated 1258, but thereafter references in Latin, French, German, English and other European languages become quite frequent. In Italy it was known as the spingarda, in part of southern France as the spingula, and in England and Scotland as the springald. In Germany and parts of central Europe it was known as the springolf, though it was also given the name notstalle or noytstelle.

The medieval espringal, like the Islamic qaws al-ziyar, was superior to the Roman original in several respects, not only in relying on fewer complicated metal parts, but probably also in performance.[14] The frame was probably about 2 metres long, 1.5 metres wide and 1.5 metres high, though some might have been up to 4 metres long, and the weapon clearly came in several sizes. The best wood was German beech, though elm and oak were also used.

The most detailed illustrations of a military crane appear in the mid-13th-century French Maciejowski Bible. Here King Saul's corpse is being exposed over the walls of Baisan (Beth-shan) on a counter-weighted device with a locking mechanism at its lower end. (f.35v, Pierpont Morgan Lib, New York)

The springallis recorded in 1293 Carcassonne was, like the ballista, placed on a rotae fustae as tenendum ingenia, a wooden wheel or rotating support frame. It was powered by the elasticity of ropes or bandas which were in bundles or fasces. The stored energy of an ordinary espringal is estimated to have been around 1,800 kg, resulting in an exceptionally powerful weapon spanned by two men using levers, a 'spindle' and a 'hook' – probably indicating a screw or winch mechanism attached to an iron rod with hooks on the end to draw back the bow-string. A source from Avignon, dated 1348, refers to this mechanism as a verrolhyera cum 2 aspes pro 1 espingola, pulling device with two hooks for one espingola, while perhaps the hooks were part of a release rather than a spanning mechanism, used because the huge power of an espringal was too great for the revolving nuts used in great crossbows. Only when metalworking technology could produce reliable iron release-nuts in the mid-14th century does the older system seem to

36

14 J. Liebel, *Springalds and Great Crossbows* (Leeds 1998), passim.

The German Einede of Heinricke von Veldeke, made between 1145 and 1200, has simple illustrations which include numerous important details. Here two armoured men knock down a tower using a battering ram held, unrealistically, in their arms. Yet it has three large rings by which it would normally be hung on ropes from the interior of an armoured roof. (Ms. Germ. fol. 282, f. 46v [oben], Staatsbibliothek, Preussischer Kulturbesitz, Handschriften-abteilung, Berlin)

have faded out. Once again the Avignon source of 1348 refers to two metallic nucibus spingalarum to be made in a mould then polished. A few decades later Conrad Kyeser mentioned the use of an iron sonifer, key or trigger, to release the projectile.

Espringals shot large arrows or viretons which were sometimes called 'tongues'. These terrifying missiles were around 70–80 cm long, up to 4–5 cm broad and weighed about 1.4 kg, though there were even larger forms. Sometimes the flights were made of bronze or latten, a less brittle alloy used in the manufacture of monumental brasses. On other occasions espringals threw stones or containers of incendiary liquid.

The espringal was, in fact, primarily used to defend fixed positions. It was not, however, suitable for use at sea because the animal-hair fasces were easily damaged by damp. Some towers may have been especially designed to provide emplacements for espringals. Given the terrifying power of the weapon it is not surprising to find them covering the approaches to gates. Since the 'tongue' of an espringal could penetrate not only any existing body armour but also the largest shields that a man could carry, few attackers would willingly approach along a path covered by a loaded espringal. Around 1400 Christine de Pisan still included two or three espringals in her suggested armoury to defend a fortified place, but did not consider them suitable for the besiegers.

DROPPING DEVICES & INCENDIARY WEAPONS

Amongst those siege machines that are occasionally mentioned in the written sources, but that rarely appear in medieval manuscript and other illustrations, were what seem to have been specialised forms of military crane. They were normally used by defenders to drop assorted materials on the attackers. The term gibet may sometimes have indicated such a device, though it usually seems to have meant a simple staff-sling. One of the few detailed descriptions of such a military crane comes from the unsuccessful English siege of Scottish-held Berwick-upon-Tweed in 1319. Here the garrison still enjoyed the services of the Flemish engineer John Crabbe, who would later change sides and work for the English. He

designed incendiary bales of wood, pitch and brimstone (sulphur) bound by iron hoops which were then dropped by a movable wooden crane onto the 'sow' or armoured roof beneath which English sappers were attacking Berwick's wall. Since this armoured roof had already been damaged by stone-throwers, presumably exposing its vulnerable timber frame, the incendiaries dropped by John Crabbe's crane succeeded in driving off the English miners. Comparable devices may perhaps have been used at sea. Venetian government regulations of 1279, for example, mention that small ships must have three spotalos or 'frames' which may have been intended to drop heavy or spiked objects on an enemy vessel. Two such 'frames' were supposedly to be mounted on the poop of each ship.[15]

Incendiaries were the most 'scientific' weapons known in the Middle Ages so it is hardly surprising to find that in so-called Dark Age western Europe nothing more sophisticated than fire-arrows seems to have been used. This was, of course, not the case in the Byzantine Empire and the Islamic world. Hence the Vikings' possession of what sounds like some form of 'sticky fire' during their siege of Paris in 886 might indicate an eastern influence or even origin. Certainly Scandinavian raider-traders were then in contact with scientifically advanced Middle Eastern and central Asian cultures via what is now Russia. What is more remarkable is that the Magyar Hungarians who attacked Pavia in northern Italy in 924 were only said to have tossed lighted torches over the city wall, since the Magyars had themselves recently been allies or subjects of the Turkic Khazars, who were in turn in close cultural, political and military contact with both Byzantium and Islamic Iran. Perhaps the Magyars possessed the technology but no longer had access to the raw materials needed

Medieval western European incendiary weapons only seem to be illustrated in the form of simple burning brands, though in this 9th-century Carolingian manuscript of the Golden Psalter of St Gallen the brands seem to be on the ends of wooden poles. (Ms. Cod. 22, p.140, Stiftsbibliothek, St Gallen)

15 F.C. Lane, 'The Crossbow in the Nautical Revolution of the Middle Ages', in D. Herlihy, R.S. Lopez & V. Slessarev (eds), *Economy, Society and Government in Medieval Italy: Essays in Memory of Robert L. Reynolds* (Kent, Ohio 1969), p 163.

for such advanced pyro-technics.

In early medieval western Europe most fortifications were still con-structed of earth and timber and, as late as the 11th century, at least one wooden castle in northern France fell victim to simple fire-arrows following a long spell of hot dry weather.[16] Circumstances began to change dramatically in the 12th and 13th centuries when attitudes towards science, technology and the possibility of learning from the feared Muslim 'Saracens' changed.

When Simon de Montfort was besieging Monerve during the Albigensian Crusade, the defenders made a sortie in an attempt to destroy De Montfort's largest trebuchet. They brought with them baskets of animal fat, straw and flax and succeeded in setting fire to the machine, but they were driven off. The fire was then doused.

Specially made metal containers for incendiary material are only rarely mentioned, although the Duke of Lorraine was said

Miners working beneath an armoured roof on wheels in an early 14th-century English or French manuscript. Meanwhile the defenders try to destroy the roof with fire-brands, rocks and large pieces of pointed timber. (Les Chroniques de France, Ms. Royal 16, G VI, f. 74r, Brit. Lib., London)

to have had his smiths make such things even in the late 10th century. During the early 13th century the technology was still not always very clear. For example the French attacking Château Gaillard in 1203–04, and the Anglo-Normans defending that castle, were both said to have used titiones or torches, globati ignes, which may have been red-hot mace-heads or spherical containers for incendiary material, and pice ferventes olle, which are understood to have been pots filled with heated pitch.

Other methods of delivering fire to the enemy included wheels of burning material which were rolled down a hill, as recorded in the Baltic Crusades of the 13th century. Large arrows or bolts with burning

---

16 M. Chibnall, 'Orderic Vitalis on Castles', in C. Harper-Bill (ed), *Studies in Medieval History Presented to R. Allen-Brown* (Woodbridge 1989), p 45.

material attached, shot by great crossbows or perhaps espringals, were another alternative. In addition to the iron-hooped burning bundles dropped by cranes during one siege of Berwick, the Scots also hung blazing bundles over the sea-walls during a later siege. These were intended to stop English ships approaching the walls but the wind suddenly changed and the flames were blown back into the town, which was set on fire.

Greek Fire, as it is generally known, was probably the most feared or the most famous weapon in the armoury of the Byzantine Empire. It was soon adopted by Muslim armies and as a result was met by Mediterranean European warriors on both land and sea. When Count Hugh of Arles attacked the Muslim-

Siege scene in a late 14th-century manuscript, showing a trebuchet and a cannon being used at the same time. It took many years before the new gunpowder weapons entirely superceded earlier stone-throwing siege-machines. (Ms. Bodl. 264, f. 255r, Bodleian Lib., Oxford)

held coastal enclave of Fraxinetum in southern France, his Byzantine allies brought ships armed with such Greek Fire. The First Crusaders faced Greek Fire, also called naft by the Arabs, and were fortunate that local Christians apparently taught them how the flames could be doused with wine vinegar. The fact that the Lateran Council of 1139 forbade the use of incendiary weapons as well as crossbows against fellow Christians suggests that by then Christian armies already had access to something like Greek Fire. Perhaps it had been brought back by the Crusaders before being tried out within Europe. Some French Chansons de Geste epic poems certainly mention this weapon, particularly those poems concerning or influenced by the ethos of the Crusade. For example the mid-12th-century Roman de Thèbes described a siege in which feu grejois was mentioned twice, burning houses and citizens alike. Les Chétifs, which was written in the late 12th century, stated that fu griois was contained in 'panniers' made of bronze. More accurate Greek and Arabic sources similarly make it clear that Greek Fire was indeed propelled from syphons made of bronze.

Some cultured and literate rulers became experts in siege pyrotechnics. Geoffrey Plantagenet, the Count of Anjou, was one such enlightened and relatively learned man who consulted Book IV of Vegetius' famous late Roman military text during his siege of Montreuil-en-Bellay in 1147. He was looking for a way to stop the defenders damaging his rams and to destroy the timber revetments which they

One of the earliest medieval European pictures to include crossbows also shows two wheeled rams being pushed against the outer palisade of a fortress. It is in the Commentaries of Hayman on Ezekiel, a French manuscript made between 980 and 1010. (Ms. Lat. 123002, f.1, Bib. Nat., Paris)

erected behind breaches made by those same rams. Geoffrey himself had close family links with the Crusader states and men with names of Middle Eastern Greek or Arab origin were also in his service. Furthermore, Geoffrey was helped by a passing monk, John of Marmoutier, who probably assisted with the obscure Latin text of Vegetius. This John of Marmoutier subsequently wrote The History of Duke Geoffrey, according to which the Duke:

'ordered an iron jar, tied with iron bands and hanging from a strong chain, to be filled with the oil of nuts and the seeds of cannabis, and flax, and the openings of the jar to be sealed with a suitable iron strip, firmly locked. Moreover he ordered the filled jar to be placed in a heated furnace for a long time until the whole thing glowed with over-great heat, so that the oil bubbling inside should boil. Having first cooled the chain by throwing water over it, it was taken out again, fixed to the arm of a mangonel and with great force and care, while it was alight, was thrown by the engineers at the strong beams of the breaches. It was expelled by the impact and a fire was made by the discharged matter. Moreover the overflowing oil joined the balls of fire, supplying food for the flames. The licking flames, vomiting in an extraordinary increase, burned three houses and hardly allowed men to escape the fire.'

This was not, of course, real Greek Fire or naft as it did not contain petroleum-based naphtha, but it was remarkably similar to a recipe for incendiary devices in Marcus Graecus' book Liber Ignium.[17] Though Marcus Graecus is believed to have been writing over a century later, he also advised putting broken red brick or fired brick with linseed oil, nut oil, or oil of hemp (cannabis) seed. This mixture should be ground up, distilled and thus become the so-called 'oil of the philosophers'. The Liber Ignium or Book of Fires for the Burning of Enemies does, however, contain the first recipe for true Greek Fire in a western European text, as well as effective fuses and what might be a very primitive form of gunpowder.

By then Greek Fire was clearly being used by the Crusaders and by others within western Europe, sometimes as a fearsome anti-personnel weapon. English Pipe Roll records from the reign of King Richard I even mention 2 shillings and 6 pence being paid for pitch to make Greek Fire. Perhaps King Richard brought the recipe, or more likely Arab chemists

17 J. Bradbury, 'Greek Fire in the West', History Today, XXIX (1979), pp 327–8.

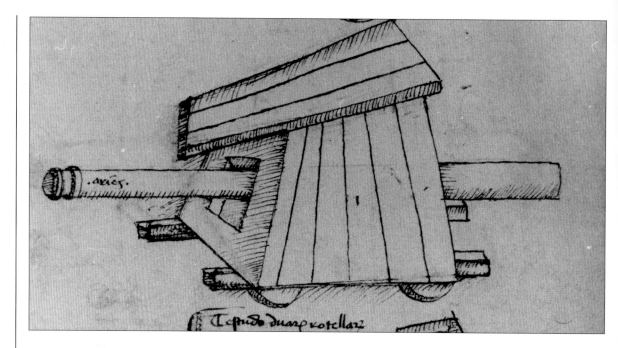

capable of making such an incendiary weapon, back from his excursion to Palestine during the Third Crusade. As a result it was used at Nottingham in 1194 and during Richard's French campaign in 1194–97. In 1216 a skilled engineer or military engineer helped the defenders of the castle of Beaucaire on the river Rhône destroy the besiegers' wooden chatte or armoured roof by using 'a pot filled with alquitran'. Apparently the chronicler misunderstood a word of Arabic origin, for this alquitran was none other than a grammatically incorrect plural of the Arabic word al-qidr meaning a large form of incendiary grenade. The Sienese defenders of Montefollonica used Greek Fire against attacking troops from Orvieto in 1229 and the army of Archbishop Konrad tried less successfully to put Greek Fire in deep bottomed wine-barges which they hoped would burn other ships defending the river-wall of Cologne in 1252. The fire, however, was so intense that it burned through the barges and sank them, spilling the remaining Greek Fire into the river before reaching its intended target. Perhaps the Archbishop's engineers were not yet used to the ferocity of Greek Fire.[18]

As was also the case in the Middle East, the first European uses of gunpowder or of a primitive mixture which incorporated sulphur and saltpetre were still described as Greek Fire. A Burgundian expert named Jean de Lamouilly who was in English service during the siege of Stirling Castle, spent 2 shillings on pots to contain such an incendiary mixture with sulphur and saltpetre which was then probably thrown by a mangonel or trebuchet. King Edward III of England also found an expert who made a Greek Fire 'dragon' during his siege of Tournai in 1340. It was a success but after the King paid the man a great sum of money to make another, he fled – with the money – supposedly because he could not produce a second 'dragon'.

Rams were normally mounted within a protective structure so that the men swinging the ram were reasonably safe from enemy fire. The areis or ram illustrated in Mariano Taccola's De Machinis of 1449 has four wheels to enable it to be moved against an enemy wall. (Cod. Lat. Mon. 28,800, f.21v, Staatsbib. Munich)

18 M. Toch, 'The Medieval German City under Siege', in I.A. Corfis and M. Wolfe (eds), *The Medieval City under Siege* (Woodbridge 1995), pp 41–42.

BIBLIOGRAPHY

M. Berthelot, 'Histoire des Machines de guerre et des arts méchaniques au Moyen Age', *Annales de Chimie et de Physique*, 6 ser. XXIV (1891) 433-521, & 7 ser. XIX (1900) 289–420.

R.C. Brown, 'Observations on the Berkhamstead Bow', *Journal of the Society of Archer Antiquaries*, X (1967) 12–17.

D.J. Cathcart King, 'The Trebuchet and other siege engines', *Château-Gaillard*, IX-X (1982) 457–469.

I.A. Corfis & M. Wolfe (eds), *The Medieval City under Siege* (Woodbridge 1995) 35–48.

G. De Poerck, 'L'artillerie a resorts medievales. Notes Lexicologiques et Étymologiques', *Bulletin Du Cange*, XVIII (1943–44) 35–49.

K. De Vries, *Medieval Military Technology* (Peterborough, Ontario 1992).

J.F. Finó, 'Machines de jet médiévales', *Gladius*, X (1972) 25–43.

J.F. Finó, 'Origine et puissance des machines a balancier medievales', *Société des antiquités nationales*, ns XI (1972).

G.H. Fowler, 'Munitions in 1224', *Publications of the Bedfordshire Historical Record Society*, V (1920) 117–132.

A.Z Freeman, 'Wall-Breakers and River-Bridgers: Military Engineers in the Scottish Wars of Edward I', *Journal of British Studies*, X (1971) 1–16.

C.M. Gillmor, 'The Introduction of the Traction Trebuchet into the Latin West', *Viator*, XII (1981) 1–8.

A.R. Hall, 'Guido's Texaurus, 1335', in B.S. Hall & D.C. West (eds.), *On Pre-Modern Technology and Science. A Volume of Studies in Honor of Lynn White Jr.* (Malibu 1976) 11–35.

P.V. Hansen &. Rayce, 'Reconstructing a Medieval Trebuchet', *Military Illustrated*, XXVIII (Aug. 1990) 9–11 & 14–16.

P.V. Hansen, 'The Witch with Ropes for Hair', *Military Illustrated*, XLIV (Apr. 1992) 15–18.

D.R. Hill, 'Siege craft from the sixth to the tenth century' in M.W.C. Hassall (eds.), *De Rebus Bellicis: part 1. Aspects of De Rebus Bellicis*; Papers Presented to Professor E.A. Thompson. B.A.R. International Series 63 (Oxford 1979) 111–117.

J. Liebel, *Springalds and Great Crossbows* (Leeds 1998).

L.V. Marvin, "Men famous in combat and battle": common soldiers and the siege of Bruges 1127', *Journal of Medieval History*, XXIV (1998) 243–258.

G.J. Mot, 'L'arsenal et le parc de matériel à la Cité de Carcassonne en 1293' *Annales du Midi LXVIII* (1956) 409–418.

R. Nicholson, 'The Siege of Berwick, 1333', *Scottish History Review*, XL (1961) 19–42.

R. Rogers, *Latin Siege Warfare in the Twelfth Century* (Oxford 1992).

G. Scaglia, Mariano Taccola, *De Machinis: The Engineering Treasise of 1449* (Wiesbaden 1971).

A. Taylor, 'Master Bertram: Ingeniator Regis', in C. Harper-Bill (edit), *Studies in medieval history presented to R. Allan-Brown* (Woodbridge 1989) 289–315.

COLOUR PLATE COMMENTARY

A: BATTERING RAM USED AGAINST ST BERTRAND DE COMMINGES DURING A MEROVINGIAN FRANKISH CIVIL WAR IN 585

In 583 Gundovald, a member of the Frankish royal family, returned to Gaul from exile in the Romano-Byzantine Empire and tried to establish his rule over the Merovingian Frankish kingdom. The result was a civil war within the Merovingian state which concluded with the siege of Convenae, now known as St Bertrand de Comminges, in the Pyrenean foothills of southern France. This little-known siege involved many aspects of Late Roman strategy, military equipment and siege technology. The attackers brought various forms of light siege-engines with them, probably including onagers, but these were not much use against the hilltop fortifications of Convenae. So, according to Gregory of Tours, who chronicled the siege, the besiegers built 'new machines', novae machinae, including powerful rams, arietes, mounted on wagons 'covered with shields'. This probably meant that roofs were erected over the wagons, made of wickerwork (cletellum) on a frame covered with planks (axes). Although there was no mention of wetted animal hides as a protection against fire, these are likely to have been laid over the flexible wickerwork while the rams themselves were probably slung from ropes attached to the roof frame. Modern calculations estimate a need for an impact of 1.0–1.75 tonnes per square centimetre to fracture the granite facing of Convenae's wall. The resulting ram was, perhaps, almost 10 metres long, 33 cm wide and weighed rather more than 700 kg. Rather than having some metallic 'ram's head' mounted on the end, which would have been liable to fracture, the point may have been given a sharpened iron tip or have been regularly re-sharpened like a gigantic pencil. It could not simply have been swung back and forth, or the tip would strike the wall or gate at the end of its arc with little momentum left. Consequently the men inside, and perhaps others behind the ram, may have hauled it back as far as they could, before releasing their hold at a given signal. Under such circumstances large wooden chocks or boulders must have been placed in front of and behind the wheels. To operate the ram effectively there must also have been a man in charge, giving orders and a signal to release the log.

B: SIEGE TOWER USED AT THE SIEGE OF VERDUN IN 985

As the Carolingian dynasty tottered to its fall, King Otto III of Germany tried to interfere in French affairs by supporting Archbishop Adalbéron of Reims' efforts to install his own nephew as the Bishop of Verdun. This resulted in King Lothair of France besieging Verdun. During this relatively brief campaign the French king's army built a movable wooden siege tower which was dragged close to the fortified wall of Verdun by oxen. To stop the oxen being panicked by enemy fire, the French used ropes through pulleys attached to stakes or tree-stumps close to the moat and wall of Verdun. Consequently the oxen were moving away from the enemy as they pulled the siege tower towards the fortifications. Because Verdun was on a river that was a major artery of trade, there was probably considerable nautical knowledge in the area, including skill with ropes and pulleys. Hence it is

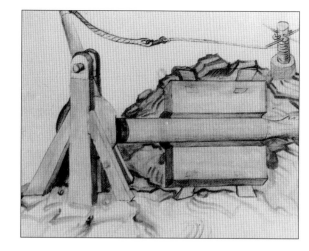

ABOVE **Boring machines are occasionally mentioned in medieval written texts, but rarely appear in illustrations. The pile-driven ram shown here comes from a 15th-century copy of Konrad Kyeser's Bellifortis, first written in the late 14th century. (Neidersachsische Staats- und Universitäts-bibliothek, Göttingen)**

BELOW **Here the Crusaders use a wooden siege tower to attack the fortified town of Emmaus in a French manuscript of around 1230. It seems to incorporate an assault bridge. Ladies taunting the tower's crossbowman from the upper wall are mentioned in several accounts of medieval sieges. (William of Tyre's Histoire de Jerusalem, Ms. Fr. 2630, Bib. Nat. Paris).**

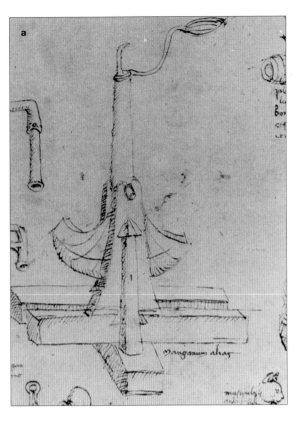

a

b

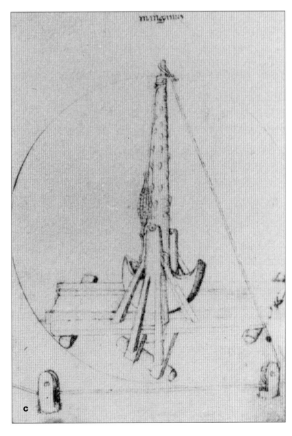

c

By the time Mariano Taccola wrote his engineering treatise De Machinis in 1449, trebuchets and mangonels had been largely superceded by cannon and the terminology of outdated weapons was also becoming confused. Nevertheless, Taccola's drawings provide some of the most realistic illustrations of such siege-machines: a – manganum alias; b – brichola, c – manganus, which seems designed to be operated from a distance. (Cod. Lat. Monacensis 28800, f.18v, Staatsbib., Munich; Ms. Palat. 766, Book IV, ff. 66v-68r., Bib. Laur., Florence)

possible that pulleys were added to the ropes to make the task easier for the oxen. This reconstruction of the Verdun siege-tower is based upon a small prefabricated timber tower which is still embedded within a medieval stone tower in the Rhineland castle of Nollich, as well as on the structure of the earliest wooden churches in Scandinavia, and surviving medieval timber bell-towers or belfries.

C: 'WOMEN-POWERED' MANGONEL USED IN THE DEFENCE OF LE CASTILLON IN 1115

This episode is drawn from the autobiographical Memoires of Abbot Guibert de Nogent. King Louis the Fat (Louis VI) had permitted the citizens of Amiens to form a commune but this was opposed by Count Enguerrand, who maintained that it undermined his rights in the surrounding county. What followed was a series of shifting alliances and small-scale fighting which culminated in King Louis besieging Adam de la Tour in the tower of Le Castillon, occupying the site of the present Hôtel de Ville in Amiens. To quote Guibert de Nogent:

'The next day huge siege towers were brought up to the

wall of Le Castillon, as it is called, and knights were assigned to them. Those of the castle had earlier protected themselves with curtain walls to prevent the taking of the heart of their defences … Meanwhile the people of the castle allowed them [the King's troops] to approach the walls and to move up the towers. When they were set in place a man named Aleran [one of the defenders], who was very skilled in these matters, placed opposite them two catapults [actually man-gonels], which he had built, and set almost four-score women to throwing the stones he had piled up. The knights inside also duelled hand to hand with the assailants [in the siege towers]. And while the men defended their ramparts with the spirit of Achilles, the women with equal courage hurled stones from the catapults and shattered both of the towers … Seeing that they were beaten, the [King's] soldiers perched in the wooden towers began to retreat, and at once the rest followed them.'

The two mangonels designed and built by Aleran were operated by 80 women – 40 to each machine – making two teams of 20 which worked in rotation. While the women pulled the ropes a skilled specialist such as Aleran himself was responsible for loosing the sling with its stone. The mangonel in this reconstruction is based partly upon medieval western European pictorial sources, and partly on a detailed written description of what was known in the Islamic Middle East as a 'Frankish' form of manjaniq or mangonel.

D: ARMOURED ASSAULT-BRIDGE USED AT THE SIEGE OF CREMA IN JANUARY 1160

The siege of Crema was a major event during the Emperor Frederick Barbarossa's northern Italian campaign of 1158–62 against a league of Italian city-states. On 7 July 1160 Barbarossa's army besieged the small but strongly defended city of Crema, which was defended by double walls and a

A stylised illustration of a movable siege tower appears in the early 14th-century Spanish Gran Conquista de Oltramar manuscript. Note the exposed ladder at the back and timber crenellations on the top. (Bib. Nac., Ms. 195, Madrid)

water-filled moat. Amongst the siege engines constructed by Imperial forces were two armoured roofs, one of which went ahead of a moveable siege-tower to clear the ground, fill the moat and lay down rollers for itself and the tower. The filling of Crema's moat was done by pushing 200 earth-filled barrels into the water, plus 2,000 cartloads of gravel. The other armoured roof seems to have been fitted with a ram which damaged part of Crema's wall.

The Emperor was now helped by the leading military engineer of the city who changed sides. This Marchesius knew the defences in detail and constructed a remarkable armoured bridge with which to place an assault force on the weakest part of the fortified wall. The supporting structure of this assault bridge was 50 metres high and enabled a bridge, over 20 metres long and 3–5 metres wide, to be lowered onto Crema's fortifications. It was covered by an armoured roof of interwoven osiers and animal hides. Approximately half of this bridge could be thrust forward, the other half presumably serving as a counterweight to keep the structure stable. Given the traditional role of sailors in the building and operation of such siege machines in Italy, it seems likely that the bridge pivoted around a central balancing point somewhat like the yardarm of a sailing ship.

The movable siege tower, to which the assault ladder was eventually attached, was described by an eye witness named Vincent of Prague. It was made of oak and was six stories high. The lower storey was said to be as high as Crema's wall and contained another bridging device which did not, however, prove a success. This tower was moved on rollers and was also protected by osiers and hides on three sides. The tower's horizontal lower frame was 'laid out like a carriage' (in modum rhede), which might indicate that the beams extended to the rear to make steering easier. When the engineers first tried to lower or swivel Marchesius' bridge, they found that its armoured roof got in the way and so this was removed. Instead the movable siege tower was brought to the side of the bridge's supporting tower, perhaps to lash both structures together and enable crossbowmen on the siege tower to provide covering fire for those using the bridge. Although the attackers failed to take possession of Crema's wall, the citizens decided that their position was untenable and so surrendered.

E: CRANE TO DROP MISSILES USED BY THE SCOTS DEFENDING BERWICK AGAINST THE ENGLISH IN 1319

Before King Edward I of England started to interfere in Scottish affairs Berwick-upon-Tweed was a prosperous frontier town within the Kingdom of Scotland. Seized by the English in 1296, its fortifications were hurriedly strengthened but they remained rather low and not very strong. In 1318 the Scots regained Berwick and the following year the troops of Edward II tried to retake it during a 10-day siege. John Crabbe, a Flemish military engineer in the service of the Scots, was in charge of the technical aspects of the defence. At one point he made incendiary bales of wood, tar, pitch and brimstone bound with iron hoops which were then dropped by a crane onto the armoured roof used by the English to protect miners trying to undermine the walls. This roof had already been damaged by the Scots' stone-throwing machine, perhaps exposing the timbers and making them vulnerable to incendiary attack. The purpose of Crabbe's crane was to place incendiary bales accurately at some distance from the base of the wall, but the crane itself would almost certainly have been on the ground inside the wall, rather than being on the parapet or walkway. It proved a success and the English siege of Berwick failed.

F: LOADING ESPRINGALS ONTO A FRENCH SHIP BOUND FOR THE CHANNEL ISLANDS IN 1339

Almost as soon as the Hundred Years War broke out between England and France, the French seized the island of Guernsey in 1338, including Castle Cornet, which was the only real fortress on the island. Nevertheless, English forces were still active in the Channel Islands and so the French sent reinforcements. The surviving records of the Clos de Galées in Rouen state that the additional military equipment sent to Guernsey included material aboard a ship commanded by a sergeant-at-arms named Johan l'Alemant. This French ship was loaded at the quayside of Rouen on 20 January 1339. Its full cargo included armour, weapons, shields with the arms of France as a small heraldic device, 80 small crossbows, nine large two-feet crossbows, three heavy crossbows spanned with windlasses, one frame-mounted windlass crossbow and two espringals garnis de ij braies cordes. In other words they already had their twisted skeins of horsehair attached. The ammunition for these espringals consisted of four barrels of heavy quarrels or bolts feathered with latten, a type of brass. The quarrels in the barrels would almost certainly have been packed in bran for safe transport, since this was the normal procedure for ordinary arrows and quarrels.

G: TREBUCHET USED BY THE ARMY OF KING CHARLES III OF NAPLES AGAINST POPE URBAN VI IN THE CASTLE OF NOCERA IN 1385

The siege of Nocera took place during a crisis resulting from the Great Schism, with rival Popes in Rome and Avignon. There had also been a civil war within the Kingdom of Naples. The circumstances leading to the siege were complex, as King Charles had previously been supported by Pope Urban VI. When they quarrelled, Nocera was the nearest fortified place which Urban's followers controlled so he withdrew there in May 1384. Queen Margaret, the most powerful woman in southern Italy, refused to allow food to go to Nocera and demanded that Urban return to Naples. He in turn threatened Queen Margaret with excommunication. After a period of ill-tempered negotiations and a plot against Pope Urban by many of his own cardinals, King Charles of Naples sent the famous condottiere general Alberigo de Barbiano to besiege Nocera. A bombardment went on for 30 days and in response the Pope came to a window three or four times a day carrying a bell, a lighted torch and a Bible ('bell, book and candle') to excommunicate the besieging army. Meanwhile all messengers caught trying to get in or out of Nocera castle were tortured. One captured Papal messenger was even thrown back at Nocera by a trebuchet; his body smashing against the castle walls. To throw the unfortunate messenger the trebuchet must have been a substantial machine, such as that shown in this reconstruction. Eventually, however, a relieving army rescued Pope Urban, who retreated via Salerno to the Papal city of Benevento.

One of the trebuchets illustrated in the early 15th-century Göttingen version of Konrad Kyeser's Bellifortis is regarded as the best and most reliable there is. Its counterweight box is disproportionately small and some of the timbers correspondingly large, especially the virga or beam-sling itself. Nevertheless, the overall proportions are reasonable and the picture also incorporates several very important details. (Neidersachsische Staatsbibliothek, Göttingen)

INDEX

Figures in **bold** refer to illustrations